HOLY HOUR
IN UNION WITH MARY

Compiled and edited by
H. E. Brown

Leonine Publishers
Phoenix, Arizona

IMPRIMATUR

✠ Daniel Cardinal DiNardo
Archbishop of Galveston-Houston
June 3, 2020

Published by

Leonine Publishers LLC
Phoenix, Arizona, USA

ISBN-13: 978-1-942190-62-2
10 9 8 7 6 5 4 3 2 1

Visit us online at www.leoninepublishers.com
For more information: info@leoninepublishers.com

CONTENTS

FOREWORD

"Rejoice always, pray without ceasing, give thanks in all circumstances; for this is the will of God in Christ Jesus for you."
(1 Thess. 5:16-18)

It is truly our joy, as followers of Jesus Christ, to worship God, in His Most Holy Sacrament of the altar in unity with the angels and saints, and with our Mother—Immaculate Mary.

Kneeling in front of our God, we would like to offer ourselves to the Lord of all creation. Our beloved Mother Mary comes with help to us. We can repeat after her, and in unity with her, we may say our own Magnificat—*"my soul proclaims the greatness of the Lord."*

This booklet may be a great help to us in worshiping God during Holy Hour in community or in silent prayer of our own. Let's open our hearts, our minds, and our lips, to give thanks, to honor One God in His Holy Trinity.

Fr. Martin Buntov, OFMConv
Wrocław, Poland

In the Name of the Father, + and of the Son, and of the Holy Ghost. Amen.

All:-

> *O Sacrament most holy, O Sacrament divine!*
> *All praise and all thanksgiving*
> *be every moment Thine!*

Leader:-

FATIMA PRAYERS

All:-

O Most Holy Trinity, Father, Son and Holy Ghost, I adore Thee profoundly. I offer Thee the Most Precious Body, Blood, Soul and Divinity of Jesus Christ, present in all the tabernacles of the world, in reparation for the outrages, sacrileges and indifference by which He is offended. By the infinite merits of the Sacred Heart of Jesus and the Immaculate Heart of Mary, I beg the conversion of poor sinners. (*Three times*)

Most Holy Trinity, I adore Thee. My God, my God, I love Thee in the Most Blessed Sacrament.

My God, I believe, I adore, I trust and I love Thee. I beg pardon for those who do not believe, do not adore, do not trust and do not love Thee. (*Three times*)

1

Leader:-

SPIRITUAL COMMUNION

All:-

My Lord of the Eucharist, I adore Thee in this tabernacle and in every consecrated Host all over the world. Since I cannot receive Thee sacramentally, come spiritually into my heart.

I firmly believe that Thou art present in the Host, as true God and true Man, with Thy Divinity and Humanity, with Thy Body and Soul, with Thy Flesh and Blood. I believe this on Thy word, because Thou art eternal Truth. Make strong and real my Faith in Thee, dear Jesus.

I am sorry for all my sins; I hate and detest them all, because they have offended and wounded Thee Who are all good and worthy of all my love. I beg Thee to cleanse me of all sin.

I want Thee, my Lord, I need Thee. Come and live in me this day. From inside me radiate upon others the fullness of Thy grace and the riches and treasures of Thy Eucharistic Heart. I ask this grace of Thee in the name of Thy Blessed Mother and mine, Our Lady of the Blessed Sacrament.

Leader:-

ACT OF ADORATION

All:-

O Jesus, humbly kneeling in Thy presence and united with all the faithful on earth and the saints in heaven, I adore Thee, true God and true man, here present in the Holy Eucharist.

Grateful even to the very depths of my soul, I love Thee with my whole heart, O Jesus, Who are infinitely perfect and infinitely lovable.

Enrich me with Thy grace, so that I may never in any way offend Thee; and thus strengthened here on earth by Thy Eucharistic presence, may I merit to enjoy with Mary Thy eternal and blessed presence in heaven. Amen.

All:-

I adore Thee every moment, O living Bread from heaven,
Great Sacrament!

Leader:-

OFFERING OF THE HOLY HOUR

All:-

Most sweet Jesus, in union with Mary, I desire to make this Holy Hour. By the fervor of my love, I wish to console Thee for all the ingratitude which Thou receives in the Blessed Sacrament. I offer these prayers for the triumph of the Church, for the conversion of sinners, and for all the intentions of Thy Sacred Heart.

Angels of the tabernacle, help me so to spend this time of prayer fervently that I may console the Heart of Jesus and promote His interests throughout the world. Receive, oh Lord, my profound homage with that of the holy angels.

Jesus, Light of the world, I believe in Thee because Thou art Truth itself. Increase my Faith. I place all my trust in Thee because Thou art infinitely merciful. Strengthen my hope. I love Thee and thank Thee because Thou hast given Thyself to me in the Sacrament of Thy love. Take away from me whatever is hurtful to me and displeasing to Thee. I repent with my whole heart of ever having offended Thee. Never permit me to separate myself from Thee again. Grant that I may love Thee always and then do with me what Thou wilt. Amen.

All:-

Immaculate Virgin, pray for me to the Sacred Heart of Jesus.

****

LITANY OF LORETO

Leader:- Lord, have mercy on us.
   All:- Christ, have mercy on us.
Leader:- Lord, have mercy on us. Christ, hear us.
   All:- Christ, graciously hear us.

Leader:- God, the Father of heaven,
   All:- Have mercy on us.
Leader:- God, the Son Redeemer of the world,
   All:- Have mercy on us.
Leader:- God, the Holy Ghost,
   All:- Have mercy on us.
Leader:- Holy Trinity, one God,
   All:- Have mercy on us.

Leader:- Holy Mary,
   All:- (*After each invocation*) pray for us.
Holy Mother of God,
Holy Virgin of Virgins,
Mother of Christ,
Mother of the Church,
Mother of divine grace,
Mother most pure,
Mother most chaste,
Mother inviolate,
Mother undefiled,
Mother most amiable,
Mother most admirable,
Mother of good counsel,
Mother of our Creator,
Mother of our Savior,
Mother of mercy,
Virgin most prudent,
Virgin most venerable,

Virgin most renowned,
Virgin most powerful,
Virgin most merciful,
Virgin most faithful,
Mirror of justice,
Seat of wisdom,
Cause of our joy,
Spiritual vessel,
Vessel of honor,
Singular vessel of devotion,
Mystical rose,
Tower of David,
Tower of ivory,
House of gold,
Ark of the covenant,
Gate of heaven,
Morning star,
Health of the sick,
Refuge of sinners,
Comforter of the afflicted,
Help of Christians,
Queen of angels,
Queen of patriarchs,
Queen of prophets,
Queen of apostles,
Queen of martyrs,
Queen of confessors,
Queen of virgins,
Queen of all saints,
Queen conceived without original sin,
Queen assumed into heaven,
Queen of the most holy Rosary,
Queen of families,
Queen of peace,

Leader:- Lamb of God, Who takest away the sins of the world,
    All:- Spare us, O Lord.
Leader:- Lamb of God, Who takest away the sins of the world,
    All:- Graciously hear us, O Lord.
Leader:- Lamb of God, Who takest away the sins of the world,
    All:- Have mercy on us.

V. Pray for us, O holy Mother of God,
R. That we may be made worthy of the promises of Christ.

Leader:- Let us pray:- Grant, we beseech Thee, O Lord God, unto us Thy servants, that we may rejoice in continual health of mind and body; and, by the glorious intercession of blessed Mary ever Virgin, may be delivered from present sadness, and enter into the joy of Thine eternal gladness. Through Christ our Lord.

All:- Amen.

All:-

Virgin most holy, by thy holy and immaculate heart, make us enter into the adorable Heart of thy Divine Son, Jesus Christ.

Leader:-

IN HONOR OF MARY, MEDIATRIX OF ALL GRACES

All:-

O Lord Jesus Christ Our Mediator with the Father, Who has appointed the Most Blessed Virgin, Thy Mother, to be our Mother also and our Mediatrix with Thee: grant that whoever draws near to Thee to beg for blessings may rejoice to receive all through her. Thou Who liveth and reigneth with Thee in the unity of the Holy Ghost, one God, now and forever. Amen.

All:-

> ***O** Heart Most Pure of the Blessed Virgin Mary,*
> *obtain for me from Jesus a pure and humble heart.*

Leader:-

ACT OF REPARATION

All:-

Sweet Savior Jesus, hidden in the Holy Eucharist, showering on us continually the wonderful treasures of Thy Sacred Heart, and receiving in return so much coldness and indifference, I adore Thee and I love Thee. From the humble tabernacle which Thou hast chosen for Thy dwelling place, from this altar on which Thou daily offers Thyself in the Mass, I beg of Thee to accept my act of reparation.

For the carelessness of Catholics in receiving the Sacraments, I ask pardon and make reparation.

For the wanderings of our mind and heart during Holy Mass, I ask pardon and make reparation.

For our want of preparation in receiving the Sacrament of Thy love and our poor thanksgiving, I ask pardon and make reparation.

For the blasphemies of sinners against Thee and Thy Blessed Mother, I ask pardon and make reparation.

For all our sins of pride and sensuality, and for the bad example we have given, I ask pardon and make reparation.

For the sins of our past life, and for all the sins of which we have been the cause, I ask pardon and make reparation.

For the lukewarmness of those who should console Thy Sacred Heart, I ask pardon and make reparation.

O Love neglected! O Goodness but too little known!

Jesus, would that I could offer Thee an act of reparation equal to the outrages committed against Thee! In atonement for the bitterness which Thou wert made to feel in the depths of Thy Sacred Heart, accept the love of Thy holy angels, the sufferings of the martyrs, and the prayers and penance of Thy saints and of all fervent souls.

Sacred Heart of Jesus, be our all-powerful reparation to the Blessed Trinity, since in Thy tabernacle Thou art always living to make intercession for us. Amen.

All:-

O Jesus in the Blessed Sacrament, have mercy on us!

Leader:-

ACT OF REPARATION TO THE IMMACULATE HEART OF MARY

All:-

Most Holy Virgin, and our Mother, we listen with grief to the complaints of thy Immaculate Heart, surrounded with the thorns which ungrateful men place therein at every moment by their blasphemies and ingratitude. Moved by the ardent desire of loving thee as our Mother and of promoting a true devotion to thy Immaculate Heart, we prostrate ourselves at thy feet to prove the sorrow we feel for the grief that men cause thee and to atone by means of our prayers and sacrifices for the offenses with which men return thy tender love.

Obtain for them and for us the pardon of so many sins. A word from thee will obtain grace and forgiveness for us all.

Hasten, O Lady, the conversion of sinners that they may love Jesus and cease to offend God, already so much offended, and thus avoid eternal punishment.

Turn thine eyes of mercy toward us so that hence forth we may love God with all our heart while on earth and enjoy Him forever in heaven. Amen.

All:-

Sweet Heart of Mary, be my salvation.

Leader:-

ACT OF CONSECRATION TO
MARY IMMACULATE

All:-

O Immaculata, Queen of heaven and earth, refuge of sinners and our most loving Mother, God has willed to entrust the entire order of mercy to thee. I, a repentant sinner, cast myself at thy feet, humbly imploring thee to take me with all that I am and have, wholly to thyself as thy possession and property. Please make of me, of all my powers of soul and body, of my whole life, death and eternity, whatever most pleases thee.

If it pleases thee, use all that I am and have without reserve, wholly to accomplish what was said of thee: "She will crush your head," and, "Thou alone hast destroyed all the heresies in the whole world." Let me be a fit instrument in thy immaculate and merciful hands for introducing and increasing thy glory to the maximum in all the many strayed and indifferent souls, and thus help extend as far as possible the blessed kingdom of the most Sacred Heart of Jesus. For wherever thou enters thou obtains the grace of conversion and growth in holiness, since it is through thy hands that all graces come to us from the most Sacred Heart of Jesus.

V. Allow me to praise thee, O Sacred Virgin.

R. Give me strength against thy enemies.

St. Maximilian Maria Kolbe

All:-

Sacred Heart of Jesus, I give myself to Thee through Mary.

******

THE HOLY ROSARY

Leader:-

THE APOSTLES' CREED

I believe in God the Father Almighty, Creator of heaven and earth; and in Jesus Christ, His only Son, our Lord; Who was conceived by the Holy Spirit, born of the Virgin Mary, suffered under Pontius Pilate, was crucified; died, and was buried. He descended into hell; and on the third day He arose again from the dead; He ascended into heaven, and sitteth at the right hand of God, the Father Almighty; from thence He shall come to judge the living and the dead.

All:-

I believe in the Holy Ghost, the holy Catholic Church, the communion of saints, the forgiveness of sins, the resurrection of the body, and life everlasting. Amen.

1 Our Father – 3 Hail Marys – 1 Glory be to the Father, etc.

Leader:-

THE JOYFUL MYSTERIES

The First Joyful Mystery- The Annunciation

PRAY THIS DECADE TO GROW IN THE VIRTUE OF PURITY

While praying this mystery, unite yourself to Mary's purity which led to her interior disposition of obedience and her submissiveness to God's Will. Each **"Hail Mary"** we pray in this decade should increase our desire to say "yes" to God in all that He asks us to do.

11

Mary's "fiat" gave us the Holy Eucharist as the Body of Our Lord Jesus Christ was formed from His Immaculate Mother at the moment she consented to become the spouse of the Holy Ghost. It is in that Body that He remains with us in the Most Blessed Sacrament.

Mary, at the moment of the Incarnation, thou became the first tabernacle on earth containing the presence of the God-Man, Jesus Christ. Thou, Joseph, and the hosts of angels were chosen to be the first adorers of the hidden God.

Throughout time, Our Lord through His Church has willed that His chosen people continue to adore Him in the Most Blessed Sacrament.

BLESSED SACRAMENT PRAYER

All:-

Aware of Thy loving Presence in the Most Blessed Sacrament, Jesus, we unite ourselves to Mary and offer Thee her perfect devotion to make up for our lack of response in doing Thy Will. May we become truly docile and prompt in carrying out Thy Holy Will at all times. Amen.

1 Our Father – 10 Hail Marys – 1 Glory be to the Father, etc.

All:- (At the close of the decade)

O my Jesus, forgive us our sins, save us from the fire of hell, lead all souls to heaven, especially those most in need of Thy mercy.

Leader:-

The Second Joyful Mystery-
The Visitation

PRAY THIS DECADE TO GROW IN THE
VIRTUE OF CHARITY

While praying this mystery, unite yourself to the virtue of charity, the Blessed Virgin Mary practiced in visiting her cousin Elizabeth. Charity must first start in the home and then reach out to everyone else. Each **"Hail Mary"** we pray in this decade should lead us to an increase in our good works toward the members of the Mystical Body of Christ.

The Blessed Virgin Mary helped Elizabeth in her time of need and so now she reaches out to us with Her Divine Son in the Most Blessed Sacrament, where we can gain our strength to help others in the name of her Son.

As Saint John the Baptist recognized Our Lord Jesus Christ hidden in the womb of the Blessed Virgin Mary, we, too, now recognize Our Lord Jesus Christ hidden in the Most Blessed Sacrament, the mystery of our Faith.

BLESSED SACRAMENT PRAYER

All:-

Jesus, we unite ourselves to the perfect charity of Mary and pray, through her intercession, that our charity may become more perfect. By the infinite power of Thy Eucharistic Love, we beg Thee to conquer and cast out every doubt, fear, and anxiety that we have so that Thy charity and peace may reign in our hearts. Amen.

1 Our Father – 10 Hail Marys – 1 Glory be to the Father, etc.

All:- (*At the close of the decade*)

O my Jesus, forgive us our sins, save us from the fire of hell, lead all souls to heaven, especially those most in need of Thy mercy.

Leader:-

The Third Joyful Mystery-
The Nativity

PRAY THIS DECADE FOR GROWTH IN THE SPIRIT OF POVERTY

While praying this mystery, unite yourself to Mary's and Joseph's spirit of poverty as they and the Divine Infant Jesus shared a stable with the animals of the fields. Poverty is not only the lack of external comforts, as in the case of the Holy Family, but a spirit of detachment from possessions. Each **"Hail Mary"** we pray in this decade should increase our desire to grow in spiritual wealth.

We pray for Mary's spirit of poverty. May we strive to become so spiritually detached that Our Lord Jesus Christ in the Most Blessed Sacrament becomes our greatest treasure.

When the shepherds and Magi came to adore the Infant Jesus, they found the Blessed Virgin Mary holding Him in her arms, showing Him to His first public adorers. We are as privileged in being called to adore Him today by attending Mass and receiving His Body, Blood, Soul, and Divinity in Holy Communion and by adoring His Real Presence in the Most Blessed Sacrament by making a Holy Hour of adoration.

BLESSED SACRAMENT PRAYER

All:-

Divine Jesus, we unite ourselves to the perfect adoration of the Blessed Virgin Mary and offer Thee all the adoration she gave to Thee on that first Christmas night when she held Thee in her arms. We thank and praise Thee with all the affection of the Blessed Virgin Mary for becoming one like us, in every way but sin, and for continuing Thy Sacramental Presence among us in the Most Holy Eucharist. Amen.

1 Our Father – 10 Hail Marys – 1 Glory be to the Father, etc.

All:- (At the close of the decade)

O my Jesus, forgive us our sins, save us from the fire of hell, lead all souls to heaven, especially those most in need of Thy mercy.

Leader:-

The Fourth Joyful Mystery-
The Presentation

PRAY THIS DECADE TO GROW IN THE VIRTUE OF OBEDIENCE

While praying this mystery, unite yourself to the virtue of obedience, the Blessed Virgin Mary practiced when she brought the Infant Jesus into the temple according to the Hebrew custom of the time. There was no need for Our Lord Jesus Christ, Who was to redeem all of mankind, to be "redeemed" as prescribed by the Mosaic Law and yet the Blessed Virgin Mary silently obeyed. With each **"Hail Mary"** we pray in this decade, we should ask the Blessed Virgin Mary to accept our total consecration to her and to present and consecrate us to the Sacred Heart of Jesus, as she presented and consecrated the Infant Jesus in the temple. In imitation of Mary, we too should consent to do that which is not required of us.

In union with Mary's obedience, we ask her to direct all our thoughts, desires, words and actions to the Most Sacred Heart of Jesus.

Ask Mary Immaculate to help you keep faithful to Our Lord Jesus Christ that you may find your strength and joy in His Eucharistic Love.

BLESSED SACRAMENT PRAYER

All:-

Lord Jesus, transform our weak and sinful hearts. Give us a "new heart" dedicated to obedience by giving us the dispositions of Thy Sacred Heart. We renew our total consecration to the Immaculata, Thy Most Holy Mother. Through her obedience, we offer to Thy Eucharistic Heart all that we have and all that we are. We especially pray for our priests, that they may be holy and dedicated to Thee. Amen.

1 Our Father – 10 Hail Marys – 1 Glory be to the Father, etc.

All:- (*At the close of the decade*)

O my Jesus, forgive us our sins, save us from the fire of hell, lead all souls to heaven, especially those most in need of Thy mercy.

Leader:-

The Fifth Joyful Mystery-
The Finding of Jesus in the temple

PRAY THIS DECADE FOR
FERVOR IN RELIGIOUS DUTIES

While praying this mystery, unite yourself to Mary's fervor in seeking out her Divine Child, Jesus, Who was missing for three days. Each **"Hail Mary"** we pray in this decade should increase our desire to always be united to Our Lord Jesus Christ; to never "lose" Him through committing sin and to frequent the Sacrament of Penance to ever keep that disposition.

16

The Blessed Virgin Mary and Saint Joseph sought Our Lord Jesus anxiously when He was missing for just a short time. The Blessed Virgin Mary continues to help all of mankind to find Our Lord in the Most Blessed Sacrament. She is our model; filled with love for Jesus and humility. We should join with her to help all persons find Our Lord in the Most Blessed Sacrament.

May Mary Immaculate help us to contemplate Our Lord in the Most Blessed Sacrament—to seek His mercy, wisdom, compassion, and joy.

BLESSED SACRAMENT PRAYER

All:-

Divine Jesus, through the sinless heart of Mary, we beseech Thee to make us more fervent adorers of Thy Eucharistic Presence. Thou wilt that all mankind be saved and come to the knowledge of Thy Truth. We entrust to Thy Eucharistic Heart all those who are weak in their Faith and beg Thee to keep them faithful to Thy Teachings and Truth in this life so that they may not be parted from Thee in eternity. Amen.

1 Our Father – 10 Hail Marys – 1 Glory be to the Father, etc.

All:- (At the close of the decade)

O my Jesus, forgive us our sins, save us from the fire of hell, lead all souls to heaven, especially those most in need of Thy mercy.

Leader:-

HAIL, HOLY QUEEN

All:-

Hail, Holy Queen, Mother of mercy, our life, our sweetness, and our hope! To thee do we cry, poor banished children of Eve; to thee do we send up our sighs, mourning and weeping in this valley of tears. Turn then, most gracious advocate, thine eyes of mercy toward us, and after this our exile, show unto us the blessed fruit of thy womb Jesus. O clement, O loving, O sweet Virgin Mary.

Leader:- Pray for us, O Queen of the most holy Rosary.

All:- That we may be made worthy of the promises of Christ.

Leader:- Let us pray:- O God, Whose only-begotten Son, by His life, death, and resurrection, has purchased for us the rewards of eternal salvation; grant we beseech Thee, that meditating upon these mysteries of the most holy Rosary of the blessed Virgin Mary, we may imitate what they contain, and obtain what they promise. Through the same Christ our Lord.

All:- Amen.

All:-

> *O Mary, Mother of grace and Mother of mercy,*
> *do thou protect us from our enemy,*
> *and receive us at the hour of our death.*

Leader:-

TO THE QUEEN OF THE HOLY ROSARY

All:-

O Queen of the most holy Rosary, in these times of brazen impiety, show again thy power, with the signs which accompanied thy victories of old, and from the throne where thou art seated, dispensing pardon and grace, in pity watch over the Church of thy Son, His Vicar, and every order of the clergy and laity, suffering in grievous warfare. Hasten, O most powerful destroyer of heresy, hasten the hour of mercy, seeing that the hour of justice is daily challenged by innumerable offenses. Obtain for me, the least of men kneeling suppliant in thy presence, the grace which may enable me to live a just life on earth, and reign with the just in heaven, whilst with the faithful throughout the world, O Queen of the most holy Rosary, I salute thee and cry out: O Queen of the most holy Rosary, pray for us!

All:-

> *O Mary, Queen of the clergy, pray for us;*
> *obtain for us many and holy priests.*

Leader:-

TO JESUS ABANDONED

All:-

With Mary Immaculate, let us adore, thank, implore and console, the Most Beloved and Sacred Heart of Jesus in the Blessed Sacrament.

O Divine Jesus, lonely tonight in so many tabernacles, without visitor or worshiper, I offer Thee my poor heart. May its every throb be an act of love for Thee. Thou art always watching beneath the sacramental Veils; in Thy Love Thou dost never sleep and Thou art never weary of Thy vigil for sinners. O lonely Jesus, may the flame of my heart burn and beam always in company with Thee.

All:-

> *Praise and adoration ever more be given to the*
> *Most Holy Sacrament.*

PERIOD OF SILENT ADORATION

"Speak, Lord, for Thy servant heareth."
(1 Kings 3:10)

"Lord, what wilt Thou have me do?"
(Acts 9:6)

Leader:-

TO OUR LADY OF THE MOST BLESSED SACRAMENT

All:-

Virgin Immaculate, Mother of Jesus and our Mother, we invoke thee under the title of Our Lady of the Most Blessed Sacrament because thou art the Mother of the Savior Who lives in the Eucharist. It was from thee He took the flesh and blood with which He feeds us in the Sacred Host. We also invoke thee under that title because the grace of the Eucharist comes to us through thee, since thou art the Mediatrix, the channel, through which God's graces reach us. And, finally we call thee Our Lady of the Most Blessed Sacrament because thou wert the first to live the Eucharistic life. Teach us to pray the Mass as thou did, to receive Holy Communion worthily and frequently, and to visit devoutly with our Lord in the Blessed Sacrament.

Virgin Immaculate, thou wert present at the death of thy Divine Son on Calvary, and thou offered thy immense sorrow in union with His sacrifice. Again after the Resurrection thou wert present at the real, but unbloody death of thy Son in the Holy Mass. Teach us to unite ourselves with Jesus at the Consecration as thou did; obtain for us the grace to understand the reality of the Mass; and awaken in us the desire to assist at Mass often, and even daily.

Virgin Immaculate, thy Communions were the most fervent, the most holy ever made. When thou received thy Divine Son into thy heart, thou loved Him with a love exceeding that of any other creature for his God. Teach us to make Holy Communion the center of our life, as it was of thine, so that our lives may be entirely spent in preparing for the coming of Jesus in Communion, and in thanking Him for the gift of Himself to us.

Virgin Immaculate, after the Ascension of Jesus into heaven, thou found consolation in thy separation from Him by visiting Him often in the Blessed Sacrament. Obtain for us the grace to be always conscious of His presence in the tabernacle, and to visit Him often as thou did, especially when we are troubled, lonely, and afraid, in pain of body or mind. Teach us to remember that He is always there, ready to listen to us, to guide, protect and console us.

Virgin Immaculate, thou art the perfect model adorer of the Blessed Sacrament. Thou adored Jesus in the little white Host with the same faith, reverence and wonder with which thou adored Him on the first Christmas night and during all the years thou lived with Him. Teach us not to forget that the small, white Host is truly our God, infinite, eternal, omnipotent. Help us to conduct ourselves at all times in His presence with the modesty and reverence we owe to our God.

Virgin Immaculate, thou gave to Jesus in the Sacred Host perfect reparation. We desire to accept our daily trials for love of Him and with thee, to console Him for the ingratitude of men and the slights and outrages He suffers daily in the Blessed Sacrament both from those who believe in Him and those who do not.

Virgin Immaculate, while the Apostles preached the Gospel, thou stayed close to thy Divine Son in the tabernacle, praying to Him for the graces they needed to convert the world. Teach us to pray before the tabernacle where Jesus waits day and night to hear and grant our petitions. Teach us to pray not only for ourselves, but also for those who do not know Him in the Sacrament of His love, that the gift of Faith may be given them, and His Eucharistic Kingdom spread throughout the world.

Virgin Immaculate, perfect lover of our Lord in the Blessed Sacrament, we ask thee to obtain for us the graces we need to become true adorers of our Eucharistic God. Grant us, we beg of thee, to know Him better, to love Him more, and to center our lives around the Eucharist, that is, to make our whole life a constant prayer of adoration, thanksgiving, reparation and petition to our Lord in the Blessed Sacrament. Amen.

V. Pray for us, O Virgin Immaculate, Our Lady of the Most Blessed Sacrament.

R. That the Eucharistic Kingdom of Jesus Christ may come among us!

Leader:- Let us pray:- Lord Jesus Christ, our King and our God, Who are true God and true Man in the Bread of the Eucharist, we beg of Thee, that, in venerating so great a mystery, we may be mindful of Thy Blessed Mother, in whose body Thou was conceived by the Holy Spirit. Grant also that we may imitate her manner of worshiping Thee in the Sacred Host, her adoration, her thanksgiving, her reparation, her prayer, so that we may see Thy Eucharistic Kingdom spread and flourish throughout the whole world.

All:- Amen.

All:-

O Virgin Mary, Our Lady of the Most Holy Sacrament, glory of the Christian people, joy of the universal Church, salvation of the world, pray for us and grant to all the faithful true devotion to the Most Holy Eucharist, that they may become worthy to receive it daily.

All:-

  Hail true Body born of Mary the Virgin.

Leader:-

CLOSING PRAYER TO THE BLESSED SACRAMENT

All:-

As this hour of adoration closes, O Jesus I renew my faith and trust in Thee. I am refreshed after these moments with Thee, and I count myself among a privileged number, even as Thy disciples were, who shared Thy actual presence.

Realizing that my visit to Thee is of little avail unless I try to live a better life and set a better example, I am resolved to go forth again to my duties and my concerns with a renewed spirit of perseverance and good will. In my daily life I will try to love and serve God well, and love my neighbor also, for these two things go together. I will try to be a true disciple, indeed. Help me, O Jesus, in this my resolution.

Bless me, dear Lord, before I go. And bless not me alone, O Lord, but all as well who are here present, and all who could not come, especially the sick and the dying. Bless our homes and all the children there. Bless all our life and the hour of our death.

Grant rest to the souls of the faithful departed, and bring them into the light of Thy divine glory. So may we who have worshiped Thee and been blessed by Thee here on earth, come to behold the radiant glory of Thy unveiled countenance in heaven forever and ever. Amen.

All:-

> *Sacred Heart of Jesus, Thy Kingdom come!*
> *Immaculate Heart of Mary, triumph and reign!*

Leader:-

FOR THE INTENTIONS OF THE HOLY FATHER TO GAIN THE INDULGENCES OF THE HOLY HOUR

1 Our Father – 1 Hail Mary – 1 Glory be to the Father, etc.

-------- * --------

All:-

> *O Sacrament most holy, O Sacrament divine! All praise and all*
> *thanksgiving be every moment Thine!*

All:-

In the Name of the Father, + and of the Son, and of the Holy Ghost. Amen.

-------- * --------

HOLY HOUR INDULGENCE

All those who assist at the Holy Hour of Adoration gain a Plenary Indulgence under the conditions of Sacramental Confession, Eucharistic Communion, and prayers for the intention of the Holy Father.

(Enchiridion of Indulgences, Vatican 1968)

Other books by H. E. Brown

She Shall Crush Thy Head:
Selected Writings of St. Maximilian Kolbe

For God Alone: The Lives of the Early English Saints:
St. Hilda and St. Elfleda of Whitby

About Leonine Publishers

Leonine Publishers LLC makes fine Catholic literature available to Catholics throughout the English-speaking world. Leonine Publishers offers an innovative "hybrid" approach to book publication that helps authors as well as readers. Please visit our web site at www.leoninepublishers.com to learn more about us. Browse our online bookstore to find more solid Catholic titles to uplift, challenge, and inspire.

Our patron and namesake is Pope Leo XIII, a prudent, yet uncompromising pope during the stormy years at the close of the 19th century. Please join us as we ask his intercession for our family of readers and authors.

www.leoninepublishers.com

www.ingramcontent.com/pod-product-compliance
Lightning Source LLC
Chambersburg PA
CBHW060548030426
42337CB00021B/4484